LIFE SKILLS

LET'S DEBATE!

Greg Paulk with
Adrianna Phillips

Heinemann Library
Chicago, Illinois

Editorial: Megan Cotugno and Harriet Milles
Design: Philippa Jenkins
Production: Alison Parsons
Picture Research: Liz Alexander
Originated by Modern Age Repro House Ltd.
Printed and bound in China by South China Printing Company Ltd.

13 12 11 10 09
10 9 8 7 6 5 4 3 2 1

Library of Congress Cataloging-in-Publication Data
Paulk, Greg.
  Let's debate! / Greg Paulk. -- 1st ed.
    p. cm. -- (Life skills)
  Includes bibliographical references and index.
  ISBN 978-1-4329-1354-0 (hc)
  1. Debates and debating. I. Title.
  PN4181.P38 2008
  808.53--dc22
                        2008020305

Acknowledgments
The author and publisher are grateful to the following for permission to reproduce copyright material: ©2008 Jupiterimages Corporation **pp. 8**, **16**; ©Alamy **pp. 25**, **40** (Frances Roberts), **38** (Uppercut Images); ©Corbis **pp. 10** (Brand X), **31** (Fotostudio FM/Zefa), **5** (Thinkstock); ©Getty Images **pp. 49** (Iconica/ColorBlind Images), **17**, **9** (PhotoDisc); ©Masterfile/Hiep Vu **p. 42**; ©Photographers Direct/Stephen Hay **p. 37**; ©Photolibrary **pp. 7**, **23** (Photolibrary/Flirt Collection/Chuck Savage), **27** (IBID); ©Rex Features **pp. 18** (Burger/Phanie), **21** (David Lapper), **29** (Paul Hawthorne).

Cover photograph of a couple arguing reproduced with permission of © Getty Images/PhotoAlto/Milena Boniek.

The publisher would like to thank Tristan Boyer Binns and Laura Hensley for their invaluable assistance in the preparation of this book.

Every effort has been made to contact copyright holders of any material reproduced in this book. Any omissions will be rectified in subsequent printings if notice is given to the publisher.

Contents

Some words are printed in bold, **like this**. You can find out what they mean by looking in the glossary.

So You Want to Debate?

When most people hear the word "debate," they think it is just another word for arguing. Debating is much more than arguing. When you argue, you usually win when the other person gives up. You win a debate by proving that your point of view is better. A debate is when opposing sides, or teams, take on an issue and use well-made **arguments** with solid **reasoning** and **evidence** to support their points of view.

Rules of Debate

There are many different types of debate (see the box to the right). Some are team events and some are individual events. They all include doing research, presenting cases, and giving speeches. Debates can be held in your classroom, at local tournaments, and at national and even international events.

Most of these debate **formats** have topics that are announced beforehand. This allows you to research and practice before the actual event. However, very few debate formats let you know which side of the topic you will be defending before the event. So, you need to make sure that you are equally prepared on both sides of the issue.

One thing common to all of these debate formats is that you give your side of the issue and then you question your opponents' side.

DID YOU KNOW?

Some of the debate formats used worldwide are: parliamentary, Model United Nations (UN), public, Australasia, policy, extemporaneous, Lincoln-Douglas, Karl Popper, Student Congress, European Youth Parliament, moot court, and mock trial—to name a few. (Turn to page 55 for information about how you can research these different formats.)

Every debate has a winner and a loser. To determine the winner, you need a judge. Sometimes this can be your debate coach, a teacher, fellow students, a parent, or a volunteer. It is the judge's role to decide which team has put forward the best arguments.

Lessons of debate

Learning to debate can teach you skills that will help you in other aspects of your life. Knowing how to create and listen to a good argument teaches you to properly research a topic and respond to everyday events. You will learn fundamentals of well-written essays that you can use in school and later in life.

To win a debate you need to know everything the other debaters might bring up. You need to know your topic from all possible angles. Learning to look at issues from all sides can also make you more open-minded and informed in your everyday life.

Debating is competitive, but it should also be fun! If you are willing to dedicate your time, you will also get the pleasure of developing your abilities and eventually mastering this important life skill.

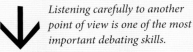

Listening carefully to another point of view is one of the most important debating skills.

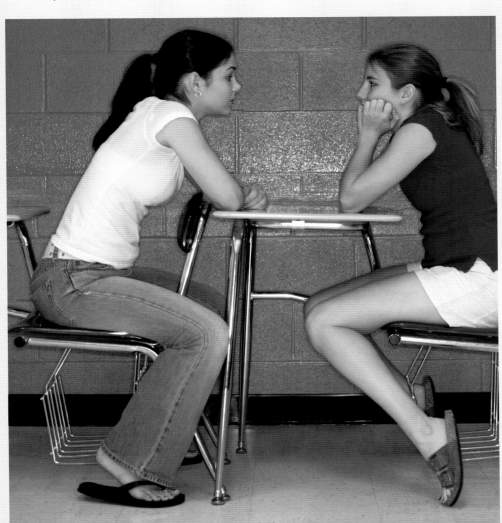

Defining and Researching a Topic

In most debate formats, topics will be given out prior to a debate tournament, often about one month beforehand. However, you will not find out which side of the topic you are arguing until shortly before the debate.

TAKING SIDES

The side that is trying to prove a statement is called the **proposition**, affirmative, or government. The opposing side can be called the **opposition** or negative. We will use the terms "proposition" and "opposition" in this book.

Let's say that you are given the topic "Dogs are better than cats." If you are on the proposition, you have to convince the judge that dogs really are better than cats. If you are on the opposition, you have to show the judge two things. First, that dogs are not better than cats, and second, why the proposition's claims are wrong.

However, you will not know ahead of time which side of the debate you will be arguing, so you need to come prepared to make any side of the argument. This preparation requires a lot of research. As you research you need to prepare logical and effective sets of arguments that will help you win your debate—on whichever side you end up taking.

Asking yourself questions

After your teacher or debate coach has provided the topic, the best way to start is to ask yourself some questions.

• CHECKLIST •

Some important questions to ask:

- What do I know about this topic?
- What do I <u>not</u> know about this topic?
- What do I need to know?
- Why is this an important topic?

An especially important question is, "Why is this an important topic?" You need to find out as much background about the topic as you can. Researching the background will allow you to explore deeper into the subject and prepare you for any surprises from your opponents.

Getting it
Right

As you ask yourself questions, it will quickly become apparent how much or little you know about a topic. Save yourself time by staying informed and up-to-date on everything around you, especially current events. Most debate topics come from recent headlines. Read newspapers and magazines and watch the news on TV. Try to get your information from a variety of viewpoints. This will give you an advantage in future debates. If you are up-to-date on your world, you will be prepared to debate many topics.

Stay current! Make sure you know about the latest news stories. You may be able to use this information to strengthen your arguments.

DEFINING YOUR TOPIC

Before you start researching, you also need to define and narrow your topic. This consists of understanding the precise meanings of every word of the topic you have been provided. This sounds as though it would be a waste of time—you would think everyone would use the obvious definitions. Right?

Wrong! Defining the topic is a strategy that is as important as good research. In fact, once you have your definition decided, your research will be easier. It will be more focused.

DEFINING WHY "Dogs are better than cats."

There are a variety of possible definitions, so it is helpful to break down this topic sentence:

"Dogs...

What kinds of dogs are we talking about—family pets, or working dogs, such as guard dogs, guide dogs, or sled dogs?

... are better ...

What do we mean by "better," and in what circumstances are they better? For instance, for families, working people, elderly people, or the environment?

...than cats."

How do dogs' qualities compare to the qualities of cats? What are the greatest strengths and weaknesses of both dogs and cats?

The reverse side

But it is not enough to prepare one side of the debate. In most debates you do not know which side you will be defending until right before the debate. Therefore, you will need to research both sides of the topic.

What if you find you are assigned the reverse side of the argument—"Cats are better than dogs"? Also, even if you are assigned the topic that dogs are better, you need to be prepared for the arguments the other side will make for cats being better.

DEFINING WHY "Cats are better than dogs."

Now break down the topic sentence supporting the other side of the argument, "Cats are better than dogs":

"Cats …"

What kinds of cats are we talking about—house cats, purebred cats, farm cats?

"… are better… "

What do we mean by "better," and in what circumstances are they better? For instance, for families, working people, elderly people, or the environment?

"…than dogs."

How do cats' qualities compare to the qualities of dogs? What are the greatest strengths and weaknesses of both cats and dogs?

DOING RESEARCH

After defining a topic, it is time to do research. The best way to start researching is to hit the books. Go to your library and get some professional help. Most libraries have computers, you can use and a trained researcher (a librarian) on hand to assist you. School librarians, teachers, or debate coaches are all fantastic resources for debaters. They can help students research almost any topic.

Using the Internet

Most students use the Internet to research a topic further. An excellent method is to use a simple search engine (such as Google, Yahoo, and msn) and type in the topic word-for-word—in this case, "Dogs are better than cats." You will probably get thousands of hits, but with a little experience you will find which sites tend to be the most useful. The table below will help you understand the function of some website **domains**.

When carrying out your research, ask as many people as you can for help. This will give you a wider range of points of view to use in your arguments.

Types of website		
Domain	**Source**	**Purpose**
.com	Companies	To help companies sell things
.org	Organizations	Usually non-commercial
.edu	Educational institutions	Educational
.gov	Governments	Government-issued information

Commercial sites (for instance, one set up by a company that sells a product you are researching) are usually very one-sided. Web logs or blogs are usually not good sites for debate facts, but they can be a good way to find links to actual data.

Taking effective notes

A vital skill is learning how to write down all the data you uncover in a meaningful way. One technique is to organize the data in the form you would use it during a debate. Perhaps draw up a sheet that looks like the example below:

Prepare your notes with your teammates so that everyone has a similar focus. But never rely on someone else's notes—always make your own notes!

Note Sheet			
Dogs		**Cats**	
For (+)	Against (-)	For (+)	Against (-)
1.			
2.			
3.			
4.			
5.			
6.			
7.			

Vocabulary

Another preparation for your debate is to learn the **specialized vocabulary** of the topic. Every topic will have vocabulary that is unique to the field. For instance, for "Dogs are better than cats," you might need to research veterinary or dog-handling terms. Terms for cats and other pets would be useful as well.

Notice these words as they pop up in your research, and then continue to investigate new and related terms even further. However, avoid the temptation to use too much specialized vocabulary during your speech. The result could be that no one, including your teammates and the judge, will understand you!

Experts and specialists

Another way to find out vocabulary terms and specific information about the topic is to contact a specialist in the field. For instance, in the case of cats and dogs, you could maybe contact local breeders or trainers. You could also ask your teacher or coach if they could invite a guest speaker who is knowledgeable about your topic to come and speak before your debate.

Fill in your note sheet with as many points as you can gather for and against each animal.

Preparing an Argument

Once you have thoroughly defined your topic and done your research, it is time to prepare your arguments.

Constructive Speeches

There are different types of speech to prepare for a debate. The first major type is called a **constructive speech**. In a constructive speech, you are trying to build a case that will support and prove your side of the topic—you are building, or constructing, your argument.

Arguing all sides

Once you know what your topic is, you need to prepare arguments that will support constructive speeches for both sides of that topic. A good argument is made up of three basic parts, called "ARE" for short:

- **A**ssertion
- **R**eason
- **E**vidence

In your debate you will need to use many different arguments to prove your case. It is not the quantity of arguments you can bring up, but rather the quality of the ones you use.

Assertion

Your **assertion** is the central claim or point of your argument. The assertion supports your side of the topic. A good assertion will be a direct statement. You don't want your assertion to be in the form of a question, because your opponents will definitely have an answer!

Let's go with the assertion:

"Dogs are better than cats."

Simply saying that dogs are better than cats does not prove anything. It is just an opinion. It is very easy to **counter** an argument like this with, "No, you're wrong."

Reason

Providing a good reason for your assertion is the second part of building a good argument. The reason is the "because" part of your statement. You need some solid reasons to show the judge why you are correct. How about:

"Dogs are better than cats because dogs can be trained to help people."

This reason helps to support your assertion and gives you direction as you find evidence. Yet you still need to add a little bit more to make this argument effective.

Think of an assertion as a wall. When you build a wall, it is important to include enough support so that your wall does not fall down. Your reasoning and evidence are the supports for your wall. Your opponents will attack your wall with **refutations** and **counterclaims**. With enough solid reasoning and evidence, no assault on your wall will be able to tear it down.

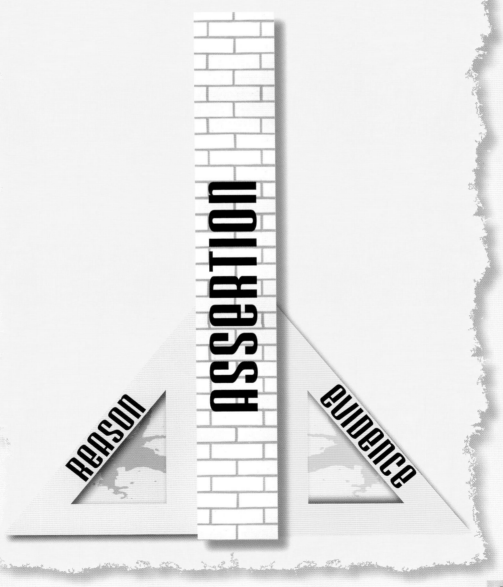

Evidence

To make a great argument, you need evidence—some real-life proof that you are not just making things up. If you are saying that dogs can be trained to help people, you need to go find some actual things that dogs can do. How do you find the evidence? You can go to the library, ask around, and use the Internet. But what might seem like good evidence is not always the best. You might say:

"Well, my brother has a dog that can fetch a newspaper."

Your opponents can then respond with the fact that your brother is only one of six billion people on the planet, and his dog is probably not representative of all dogs. And they would be correct.

Perhaps with a little more research you could say:

"The International Guide Dog Federation, with over 72 schools worldwide, trains over 1,500 dogs each year to assist the blind."

Finding several pieces of evidence for your reason will help you build an effective support. This would be pretty easy to do with the reason that dogs help people—you could mention sheepherding dogs, guard dogs, companions for the handicapped, and many more.

Some forms of debate require that you provide the source for your evidence—for example, the newspaper article you used—so make sure that you keep track of your sources.

Impact!

Having solid reasoning and evidence is not enough, however. Why should judges care about any of your arguments? You need to make it personal for judges, letting them know that this argument affects their lives. This can be a little bit more difficult to do, but it can be the difference between a good argument and a winning argument. For the argument that dogs are better than cats, you could tell a judge:

"Dogs trained to assist handicapped people help these people contribute more to society."

Getting it Right

As you do your research, look for strong opening and closing material. Quotes, statistics, and memorable phrases will hold your audience's attention.

		Definition	Example
A	Assertion	The claim or point that supports your side of the topic.	"Dogs are better than cats."
R	Reason	The "because" statement that gives support for your argument.	"Dogs are better than cats because dogs can be trained to help people."
E	Evidence	Current or historical events, studies, or data that back up or support your argument.	"The International Guide Dog Federation, with over 72 schools worldwide, trains over 1,500 dogs each year to assist the blind."

Presenting an effective argument

Once you know your major arguments, it is time to think about how you will present them. You can make a very strong argument by preparing some ideas ahead of time.

A memorable introduction

Many debaters get off to a rough start because they did not think about how they were going to start their speech. Don't make this mistake.

Find a good quote, a powerful statistic, a question (only if you intend to answer it yourself right away), or a clever saying with which you can begin your speech. Already knowing what you are going to say will make you appear more confident and prepared. You will grab the judge's attention right away.

During your introduction it is also good to give a **roadmap**. A roadmap is a brief outline of the major points you intend to make, and how they will prove your side's case. This will allow your judge to follow your side of the debate more easily. By preparing possible arguments ahead of time, you will be ready with this roadmap.

A powerful conclusion

A strong conclusion is also very important. These will be the last words the judge hears from you, so make them memorable. The famous World War II British prime minister, Winston Churchill, often said, "People don't remember speeches. They remember phrases." Thinking of a powerful final phrase ahead of time could be the winning ticket.

Preparing a Rebuttal

It is not enough to prepare arguments before a debate. You also need to be ready with refutations. To refute means to disprove an argument. You must refute all of your opponents' claims. Any points you do not refute will be considered unrefuted and therefore seen as **valid** by your judge.

Rebuttal Speeches

You can refute your opponents' points by preparing the second major type of speech, the **rebuttal speech**. The word "rebut" means to show that something is incorrect. Rebuttal speeches are used to briefly review the main points of the speeches already given and explain why your side has the winning arguments.

Rebuttal speeches let you explain to the judge why your opponents are wrong and you are right. Being on the opposition side of the topic "Dogs are better than cats," you don't just say

to the judge, "No they're not!" You have to knock down your opponents' arguments and explain clearly and simply why your arguments are better.

After your opponents have built a wall of assertions, it is your job to throw counterclaims and counter assertions to tear down that wall. As you do your research, try to think of major arguments that will be made and how you can refute them, or tear them down. To do this, you use the four-step method of refutation.

The four-step method of refutation

Step 1

"They say ..."

This is where you will let the judge know which one of the opponents' points you are going to refute. You can set up your argument with the phrase "They say," meaning your opponents make a certain claim. For example:

"They say dogs are better than cats."

"But ..."

In the next step of your argument, you make your counter assertion. You are now proposing a new and better assertion. Since this statement is presented in contrast to the opposing viewpoint, your statement will often begin with "But." For example:

> "But we disagree—cats are, in fact, better than dogs."

Step 3

"Because ..."

Now you have to provide reasoning and evidence. Without providing solid reasoning and evidence, you basically have nothing more than an opinion. The more support you can give for your side, the better off you will be. Since this statement needs to offer proof, your statement will often use "because." For example:

> "This is because cats make just as good, or even better, companions than dogs. They are cleaner and more independent. Cats groom themselves. Cats will also use litter boxes with minimal training."

Step 4

"Therefore ..."

Finally, your conclusion. You compare your point to the point you are refuting. Show that your point has more importance than your opponents'. You will also insert the impact of your argument. Since you are presenting the logic of your argument, you will often begin your statement with "Therefore." For example:

> "Therefore, while dogs may make good companions and can be taught to do tasks, cats are better companions and require less maintenance than dogs."

The four-step method in action

Using this four-step method of refutation will allow you to counter your opponents' arguments effectively. During your research, think of topics that you will need to refute and then come up with four-step refutations.

The four-step method of refutation can be used in real life, not just in a debate. If you think about most of the arguments you get into, how many of them could be settled if you had just slowed down, listened carefully, and refuted every claim? Listen carefully to others' claims. Practice finding flaws and spotting weak points. Systematic refutation can help you win almost every argument.

You can even practice the four-step method when arguing with your family—and dazzle them with your argumentation and refutation skills!

Remember, your mom can always counter your argument with the simple comment, "Because I'm your mother, that's why!" Alas, there is no known effective refutation to this!

Getting it Wrong

Many beginning debaters think that the four-step method of refutation is only for the inexperienced and try to avoid it as much as possible. Many try other complicated explanations, which often end up confusing a judge.

Experienced debaters at all levels of debate (middle school, high school, and university levels) use the four-step method. Also, using this method like a formula or recipe will let the judge know exactly when you are refuting an argument.

SO YOU WANT TO DEBATE?

1) **Preparation and knowledge are:**
   a) useful but not required.
   b) the easiest way to win a debate.
   c) necessary only for a beginner.

2) **There are two types of debate speeches:**
   a) good ones and bad ones.
   b) constructive and rebuttal.
   c) for and against.

3) **The four-step method is used:**
   a) in simple baking.
   b) to refute your opponents' arguments in a logical, precise manner.
   c) only by inexperienced debaters.

4) **Refutation is:**
   a) repeating the same argument again and again.
   b) countering your opponent's assertions effectively.
   c) good to use in a debate if you have time.

Check page 50 to see the results.

Presentation Skills

So, you have defined and researched your topic and thought about arguments and refutations. This is all extremely useful, but it is not enough just to have your work down on paper. You need to gain experience giving a performance.

Getting over nerves

Poise is an important quality for a debater. Poise is speaking and carrying yourself in a dignified, self-confident manner. In a debate you need to look confident and calm while you are standing in front of a room full of people. Poised, confident speakers will not only look better, but they will also sound better. (You may have to fake this confidence at first!)

It is hard to be poised if you feel nervous. Nervousness is often brought on by not knowing what to expect during the debate. But by doing your research and preparing your arguments and refutations ahead of time, you will feel more in control. Preparation will give you a good idea of what issues and arguments to expect from the other side.

People also often get nervous when they realize that other people are paying close attention to what they are saying. This fear is also correctable with research. If you know that what you have to say is worthwhile and backed up by sound data, then you will be happy to have listeners.

Getting it Right

The number-one fear of many people (adults and children) is public speaking. Could there be anything worse? Yes—doing it badly! If you can overcome your fears and speak in front of others, you will have accomplished a noteworthy goal. Once you realize that public speaking is a game, it is not so intimidating. It will, in fact, help you in school and later in life. Take opportunities to speak in class. This is great practice for both your presentation and debating skills.

• CHECKLIST •

To avoid getting nervous, keep in mind the following:

- Be sure you know your topic back-to-front and inside-out.

- Take a deep breath before you begin your speech.

- Focus on your judge instead of looking all around the room.

- Make yourself sound confident—your audience is more likely to listen if you smile and speak clearly.

- The night before the debate, give a few or all of your arguments in front of your parents. (No need to worry here. You are always perfect in their eyes!)

Avoid making gestures that show you are nervous, such as biting your nails or fiddling with your hair. Take deep breaths and focus.

Practice time!

The best way to calm nerves is to get plenty of practice ahead of time. Few debates are held in front of a huge audience, but for most people, any audience is too big. You may never get over your nervousness about speaking in front of others, but you can make it manageable. The best way to manage this is to practice speaking and to know your material.

Finding a test audience

Where do you practice? If you are really nervous about speaking in front of others, find a place where no one can interrupt you. A favorite hiding place for many beginners is the bathroom. Another benefit of this room is the mirror. You can practice your gestures and facial expression as well as your speaking.

You can practice in front of young children—they are usually a friendly crowd. Maybe family members or friends can be your practice audience.

Practicing with your team

As for debate practice, you need to get your fellow debaters together and start speaking. Take a practice debate seriously. When you stand up to speak make sure that your speeches fill up the correct amount of allotted time. Make sure that you practice both sides of the topic. Have your teachers or coaches observe you debating and speaking whenever possible.

Getting it Right

Debate coaches can teach you a lot, based on their own experience. Don't hesitate to go to your coaches with questions about anything, from how to research and how to make arguments to how to perform well. Listen to your coaches if they point out anything they think you should change—they know what they are talking about! Also feel free to talk to your coaches if you run into problems. For example, if you and your debate partners aren't working well together, talk to your coach about changes to the team. At the end of the debate, judges will give you constructive feedback. You'll learn valuable lessons from making mistakes and listening to judges' feedback.

A coach can help you work on your presentation skills and help you speak more effectively. Getting feedback from an experienced coach will help you polish your performance.

PERFECTING YOUR SKILLS

To be an effective debater, you must present your speech in a manner that keeps your audience interested. To do this there are several skills, **verbal** and **nonverbal**, that you will need to practice and develop.

First, keep in mind a variety of techniques and issues that are verbal, or related to speech.

Volume

Many beginning speakers are either too quiet or too loud. You need to have the appropriate volume for the room. A good way to practice this is to have a friend move around the room to see if you are too loud or too quiet as you speak.

Rate

Another concern is rate or speed. When people are nervous they tend to speak much more quickly. Often inexperienced speakers will speak so quickly that no one can possibly understand what they are trying to say. One good way to slow yourself down is never to speak when you are looking down. Most people tend to speak much more quickly when they are not looking at their audience, so try to remember not to speak when you are glancing down at your notes. Pause as you look down and then carry on speaking as you look up.

Pronunciation

Pronunciation is a problem for many public speakers. Nervousness can make you mumble! When speaking you need to make sure that everyone can understand each word that you are saying. One way to practice this is to exaggerate your lip movements. Get those lips off the teeth! Slow your speech down and actually say the words. If you need help you can practice with tongue twisters (see Tip box on page 25).

Emphasis

Using the proper **emphasis** is critical in good public speaking. You should use emphasis to stress the importance of some words. Pausing before or after a word or phrase can give emphasis.

Inflection

The worst thing you can do is to bore your judge with a **monotone** voice—and in a few cases judges have even fallen asleep! The judge will never listen to what you have to say if your voice is uninteresting.

Monotone can be fixed with **inflections**. This is making your voice louder and stronger on important points, or when countering arguments that you feel are outrageous. You can lower your voice to make sad points, or when disagreeing with shameful reasoning given by your opponents.

Practice reading your notes out loud. Make sure you read them slowly and clearly.

If you need to improve your pronunciation using tongue twisters, there is no better resource than Dr. Seuss's *Fox in Sox*.

Other favorite tongue twisters are simple phrases such as "toy boat," or "red leather, yellow leather," and "the lips, the tongue, and the teeth." Choose one of these phrases and repeat it as quickly as possible, making sure your pronunciations are perfect.

To improve inflections, recite a piece from a play that changes mood. Use the correct tone of voice to match the mood. The play *Harvey* by Mary Chase contains many scenes with changing tones, or the book *Green Eggs and Ham* by Dr. Seuss.

Word choice

Word choice is a critical part of your delivery. Don't use the same words to describe everything in your speech. Watch some television commercials to find persuasive words and phrases. Also, remember that a debate is a formal setting. You need to use proper English, not the same language you use with your friends.

Professionalism

Try to remember that really good speakers are professional. They are not pompous or on the attack. You should seem powerful as well as humble. Your power will not come from rude remarks or raising your voice, but rather from carefully chosen words.

The "one-minute speech"

A good way to rid yourself of **Amandas** (see box right) is to practice the "one-minute speech." This exercise needs a speaker and a judge with a timer. The rules are that the speaker must stand and speak on a subject for one entire minute—without using any Amandas, pausing too long, repeating him or herself, or going off the topic. If the speaker breaks any of these rules they lose, and the timer starts over with a new topic.

This might sound easy, but it will really test your skills, plus it can be a lot of fun—especially if you make it a group activity.

Getting it Wrong

"Amandas" are a common problem with all speakers. These are filler words, such as "um" and "uh". Often people use filler words when thinking out loud, as they try to find the correct word or thought.

Other Amandas are "you know," "like," "well . . . ," "anyway," "okay," "yeah," "right"—and many, many others. Sometimes it is just a really deep sigh.

Almost every single person uses Amandas in everyday speech—and we mostly don't even notice we are doing it. However, they become more noticable when someone is speaking publicly, and can be distracting and annoying for an audience. Listen to yourself speaking—you could even record yourself—and count how many Amandas you utter in a minute. Then try to cure yourself of the Amanda habit!

Eye contact

Proper eye contact is an important nonverbal skill. It is hard for a beginning speaker, but it is perhaps the most important nonverbal skill to master. If you are trying to convince or persuade an audience or judge, eye contact is critical.

Look around the room as you speak—don't look down or just focus on one spot. It may make an inexperienced speaker uneasy to look directly at the judge, but remember that a debate is a game. The only way to win this game is to convince the judge that your side is right. Making confident eye contact can make all the difference to the judge's assesment of your argument.

Good and frequent eye contact will also help with your speaking speed. If you make yourself look around, you will slow down. And remember, don't speak when looking at your notes.

Making steady eye contact is not easy if you are nervous. But looking around and making eye contact with members of the audience is a key debating skill.

Correct bad habits

Part of learning to be a good public speaker is recognizing your own bad habits and learning to correct them. We sometimes do not realize that we make certain gestures or sounds when speaking, so during practice be sure to have friends point out any bad habits to you.

Avoid making distracting movements. When you stand up to speak, do not move about. Plant your feet firmly so you do not rock back and forth.

If you have a habit of playing with your hair, tie it back. If you like to adjust the speaker's stand throughout your speech, keep your hands off it.

Do not bring distractions with you. For instance, if you have a habit of clicking your pen, leave it at your table. If you hold it while you are speaking, you could be tempted to keep clicking it. This will take the judge's attention away from your speech.

TIP

To instantly improve your posture, imagine the top of your head is attached by a string to a helium balloon. Imagine that the balloon is lifting your head and pulling your spine straight.

DID YOU KNOW?

Judges will mark you down for poor body language. Mumbling and not looking up from notes, or making nervous or distracting gestures will count against you.

All of these distractions make you seem fidgety, nervous, or unprepared. You want to remain **credible** in the mind of the judge—so stay professional.

Posture

Posture is also important. Good posture will help you with breathing, pronunciation, eye contact, and volume. Plus, standing up straight will not only make you look in control, but will command the full attention of the audience. Lift your chin slightly when you speak. This will help your voice to carry around the room—without having to shout!

Gestures

Your speech can also become more intriguing with hand gestures. This does not mean you should wave your hands all over the place during the entire speech. There are strong gestures like making a fist and using the bottom of it to impact your other outlaid hand. This gesture can be used when you are saying something important that you want to make sure the judge notices.

You can also match words with gestures. For example, if you are saying, "Our plan will make these problems go away," you can sweep your hand across to indicate the word "away." Hand motions are powerful as long as they are not overused.

Strong confident gestures can draw your audience in and make your speech more powerful.

TIME TO DEBATE!

Once you have prepared your content and presentation, it is time to debate! However, before you go off to your debate there are a few last-minute things to remember. Planning ahead will make sure you are ready for anything.

• CHECKLIST •

The night before:

- Do you have the right clothes ready? You will need to ask your teacher or coach what the required dress code is for the debate. Don't just assume normal school clothes will be okay. You also need to check with your debate team. It is good to wear something that shows you are all on the same team.
- Do you have your notes? (Never lend your notes to other people.)
- Do a last-minute practice. You can never have too much practice.
- Do you have transportation arranged? If it is a normal school day, you have no worries, but if it is a weekend event, make sure you will be able to get to where you are supposed to be on time.
- Get some sleep! Debating is heavy brainwork. It requires a lot of energy, so proper sleep is a must.

On the day:

- Get up in plenty of time. Set that alarm clock! There is no need to start the day off with extra stress.
- Eat breakfast. As mentioned before, debating is heavy brainwork and requires a lot of energy, so a good breakfast is a must.
- Do you have your notes? You can never check too many times!
- Arrive early. Too early is always better than too late.

Expect the unexpected

Make sure you have done all your preparation well before "the night before." The last thing you should do is to sit up late into the night panicking about final adjustments to your speech. A good night's sleep is essential for a good performance.

The hardest part about debating is that it is mostly **impromptu**. *Impromptu* means something that is done on the spot.

True, you have prepared your arguments and refutations, but a debate is an ever-changing performance. You have to respond on the spot to anything unexpected that your opponents might present to you. If you feel fresh and prepared you will be ready for any challenge!

You will be able to debate more effectively if you have a good night's sleep. You'll have more energy and you'll be able to think more clearly.

DEBATE FORMATS

As mentioned earlier in the book, there are a variety of debate formats throughout the world. These all feature a series of constructive and rebuttal speeches. However, there are variations when it comes to the order of the speeches, the time allowed for the speeches, and the number of teammates.

A sample debate format

To show how a sample debate format works, we will look at the Middle School Public Debate Program (MSPDP) format, which is a form of parliamentary debate (see page 52) that has been specially designed for middle school students. Other kinds of debate format may have different details, but they all use the same skills as this one.

In an MSPDP debate, there are two teams—the proposition, and the opposition. Each team has three speakers: a first speaker, a second speaker, and a "rebuttal" speaker. Each speaker makes one speech. The proposition team always begins and ends the debate.

The first two speakers on each team take turns to make constructive speeches. They will use these speeches to build positive arguments for their assertions. They will also be expected to answer questions from the opposing side during these speeches.

The final speakers on each team will make rebuttal speeches. These two speakers will summarize and reinforce their own team's arguments, and state why they should win the debate.

The burden of proof

The MSPDP works to a similar format as a legal trial. In a court of law, the "burden of proof" is put on the **prosecution**. This means that the prosecution has to prove that the **defendant** is guilty—rather than the defendant having to prove that they are innocent. In a debate, the burden of proving the original assertion is on the proposition team.

> ## TIP
>
> During a constructive speech, the opposing side can ask **Points of Information** (POIs), which are questions or quick comments used to throw the speaker off guard. If speakers are smart about this, though, they can use these opportunities to clarify a point or subject. (For more on POIs, see pages 40–41.)

The proposition team is responsible for proving that they have the best argument. Because the proposition has the more difficult job, they get to speak first and last.

The table below shows how a MSPDP debate is structured, the task of each speaker, and how much time each speaker gets to make his or her arguments.

The order of the MSPDP debate format		
Speaker	**Time Limit**	**Task**
First proposition (constructive)	5 minutes	Opens the debate with a strong case for the topic. Uses the three or four major points to provide proof for the proposition's argument.
First opposition (constructive)	5 minutes	Makes positive arguments against the proposition's assertions. Refutes the propositions major points.
Second proposition (constructive)	5 minutes	Reinforces the first proposition speaker's points and refutes the oppositions assertions.
Second opposition (constructive)	5 minutes	Reinforces the first opposition speaker's arguments against the proposition's assertions.
Opposition rebuttal	3 minutes	Refutes the proposition's main points and explains why the opposition should win the debate.
Proposition rebuttal	3 minutes	Refutes the opposition's arguments, summarizes the propositions major points, and explains why the proposition should win.

It may seem like the proposition have a strong advantage because they open and close the debate. However, if you look at the table you will see that the opposition get eight whole consecutive minutes to push their point near the middle of the debate! This gives the opposition a good chance to dominate.

THE SIX SPEECHES IN THE MSPDP FORMAT

1. First proposition constructive

The first speech, given by the first member of the proposition, is the "first proposition constructive." In other words, this is the first constructive speech given by the proposition.

This speech can last five minutes. In this speech the speaker:

- defines the proposition's topic
- gives three or four assertions with reasoning and evidence
- provides meaningful impact for all arguments
- ends with a powerful conclusion.

This speech is unique from the five others that follow because there are no refutations—it simply lays forth the argument.

2. First opposition constructive

The second speech, given by the first member of the opposition, will be the "first opposition constructive." In other words, this is the first constructive speech given by the opposition.

The speech lasts five minutes. In this speech, the speaker:

- refutes all of the proposition's points
- gives three or four assertions with reasoning and evidence
- provides meaningful impact
- ends with a powerful conclusion.

This is almost the same format as the first speech, but with the addition of refutations. The speaker should use the four-step method of refutation ("They say," "But," "Because," and "Therefore").

Getting it Wrong

A weak opening speech will be torn apart by the following speaker and will mean the rest of the team have nothing to support. It is important to choose a strong speaker to make your opening speech.

TIP

Every point needs to have added impact! Adding impact is all about making sure the judge sees how your arguments affect him or her. Add something to make the judge sit up and take notice.

3. Second proposition constructive

The third speech, given by a second member of the proposition, is the "second proposition constructive." This lasts for five minutes.

In this speech the speaker will need to support all of the points made by the first speaker from the team. The new speaker cannot just repeat the same assertions, reasons, and evidence, however. It is fine to use the same assertions, but the speaker needs to add new reasoning and evidence, and maybe also bring up one or two new points.

The speaker will need to refute all of the opposition's points as well. This is the last chance to bring up new ideas or points for the proposition.

4. Second opposition constructive

The fourth speech, given by the second member of the opposition, is the "second opposition constructive." It can last for five minutes. In this speech the speaker will need to:

- support all of the points made by the first speaker from their team.
- provide new reasoning and evidence.
- refute all of the proposition's points—from both the first and second proposition speakers.

If possible, it is best to group some of the proposition's points together, as this makes refuting them a little easier. The speaker may bring up some new points for the opposition as well.

Getting it Wrong

Some debaters stand up and read their pre-written speeches no matter what has been said in the debate before them. This makes for a really boring debate and an easy decision for the judge. It also shows that they haven't been listening properly.

TIP

Judges are responsible for timing the debate. you will need to make sure you use your time fully, but do not run over. This takes practice to get right.

5. Opposition rebuttal

The fifth speech, given by the third and final member of the opposition team, is the "opposition rebuttal." It lasts for three minutes. With this speech the speaker has the final chance to convince the judge that his or her team wins the debate.

In a good rebuttal speech, the speaker needs to bring together the main points of the proposition side and explain why they are wrong. The speaker will also need to bring together his or her team's points and explain why they are superior.

This speech should not be just a repeat of every assertion and refutation made by the speaker's side, but rather a bringing together of the entire debate to show that his or her team has obviously won.

Getting it Wrong

If rebuttal speakers have not kept track of the previous arguments and refutations, they will not be able to answer their opponent's arguments directly and this will count against them.

• **CHECKLIST** •

The rebuttal speakers need to:

- Tell the judge why their side has won the debate. Go over their side's main points. Go over the other side's main points.

- Explain their team's points. Go over the big points. Remember "quality not quantity", and add impact to every point

- Explain the other team's points. Explain why even with all of the other team's arguments, their own team should still win. (Remember to add impact.)

- In conclusion, tell the judge why their own side has won the debate. Go over their side's main points. Use impact for their final point in the debate.

The speaker tells the judge, "Our side has won this debate, because ... ," explaining the reason. A good debater will use impact to end a rebuttal speech. This means they will be sure to end with a powerful point that will stick in the judge's mind. (See the checklist above for an outline of an effective rebuttal speech.)

6. Proposition rebuttal

The last speech, given by the third and final member of the proposition team, is the "proposition rebuttal." This lasts for three minutes. This is the last speech the judge will hear in the debate. This speech follows the same format as the previous rebuttal speech, except that the speaker will also be able to refute the opposing team's last speech.

Getting it Right

In a concluding speech:

a) Give an overall view of your opponents' points.

b) Give an overall view of your team's points.

c) Explain how your points have won this debate.

d) Make a powerful concluding statement.

Taking part in regular informal debates is the best way to increase your confidence and your skills.

WHAT IS A DEBATE JUDGE LOOKING FOR?

Judges track and evaluate the arguments put forward by the members of each team. They will award points for:

- well-constructed arguments using **A**ssertion, **R**eason, and **E**vidence

- clear thinking

- quick responses to rebuttals

- good teamwork

- persuasive presentation

- good verbal and nonverbal skills.

Don't overwhelm the judge with numbers and statistics. Remember that the judge is also trying to take notes from your speech. A few strong statistics will be more memorable than a flood of data.

Your judge could be one of your teachers, your debate coach, or even a fellow student.

Questioning Your Opponent

Debates are not just about giving speeches in front of a judge. They are also about asking and answering questions. How well you are able to ask and respond to questions will make a big difference to how your performance is judged, no matter how good your speeches are.

Points of Information

In a debate there are many ways to question your opponents. Some formats have **cross-examination** rounds or periods for questions built into the format. Others, like the MSPDP format, have Points of Information (POIs).

A POI can be a statement, a question, a clarification, or even used just to interrupt the speaker's flow.

Constructive speeches have a period called "protected time" during which the speaker cannot be interrupted. This time is during the first and last minutes of the speech. But POIs can be asked during the rest of the speech, which is known as "unprotected time."

The judge will indicate when protected and unprotected time begins and ends by using a physical signal of some description—for example, slapping a table top or blowing a whistle.

To offer a POI during unprotected time, you stand up and wait for the speaker to accept or deny your request. Speakers do not have to accept a POI, but it is a good idea to accept a few. If you are planning to ask for your own POIs to be accepted, you need to take a few as well.

A POI should be 10 to 15 seconds long. If you talk for longer than this while offering a POI, the speaker should cut you off.

Getting it Right

Plan ahead with your POIs Write down the assertions you expect the other side to make, and have your questions ready.

Using POIs

When you are offering POIs, you will really benefit from having done your homework. The more prepared you are, the easier it will be to find the flaws in your opponents' arguments.

If you see that your opponents do not have evidence for one of their points, stand up and ask. If your opponents are using words that they clearly don't understand, stand up and ask for a definition. If you know the material better than the opposing side, you can run them ragged with questions. This is your opportunity to show the judge that the other team members clearly don't know what they are talking about.

With the proper questioning, you can sometimes fluster speakers so badly that they will even start arguing for the wrong side. Sidetracking speakers is also possible with an off-topic question. You can sometimes get speakers to waste their time answering a question that really has nothing to do with the debate. This does not mean you should be asking silly questions. You have to ask something that is relevant to the overall topic, but that might have nothing to do with the debate itself.

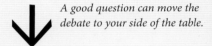

A good question can move the debate to your side of the table.

Fallacies

When you hear a **fallacy**, you need to point it out. A fallacy is faulty logic used in an argument. Even though it is faulty logic, it can still sound pretty convincing. But, if you can show the judge how your opponents are using fallacies in place of facts in these situations, you may win the debate.

There are hundreds of different fallacies, but the examples in the table below are a few of the most frequently used:

Getting it Wrong

You should never be rude or cruel to any speaker. If a speaker stammers, is exceedingly nervous, or is new to debate, you should never demean or belittle him or her. Developing a winning strategy is a good idea. Cruelty to another speaker is always wrong.

Fallacy	Example	Explanation
False **dilemma**	"You're either with me or against me."	You are only given two choices, although there are probably more.
Slippery slope	"If we let the government pass this one law, we will lose all of our rights."	Saying that if we let this one problem go, we will have worse problems later on.
Language	"Any intelligent person would see the logic of my argument [that I am right]."	Giving value to a statement by your choice of language.
Attacking the person	"She is just a child, what would she know."	Attacking the person and discounting his or her argument.
Appeal to emotion	"Children will die!"	Trying to play on the judge's emotion.
Popularity	"Everyone has one of these, so it must be good."	Exaggerating how popular something is to prove it must be good. (This is used by many advertisements.)

Flowing a Debate

Listening is one of the most important skills you can have as a debater. It is essential that you hear every point made by your team and by your opponents. As you listen, you need to have an effective system to write down what your opponents have said. With practice, you will learn what to take down and what to leave out.

Making a Flowsheet

The system of taking notes during a debate is called "flowing" a debate. It is called "flowing" because you should look at a debate as a single, continuous speech, not a series of disconnected speeches.

A **flowsheet** is a piece of paper with lines and headings. It should be a complete set of notes for the debate, not just separate sets of notes for the individual speeches. It is called a flowsheet because the speeches flow across the page.

Begin by separating a piece of paper into columns that represent the order of speeches that will be given. As we have seen, there are a variety of debate formats, all with different numbers of speeches, types of speech, and orders of speeches. Make your chart match the format you are using.

Effective note-taking can help you win a debate. Keep short notes to help you keep track of the different arguments as the debate progresses.

If you are using the Middle School Public Debate Program (MSPDP) format, for example, you will have to label the columns of your flowsheet with the order of speeches examined in the last chapter: first proposition constructive, first opposition constructive, second proposition constructive, second opposition constructive, opposition rebuttal, and proposition rebuttal.

Remember, you need to take notes on both sides of the debate, not just on your opponents. It is critical to note down what your own side has said as well, so that you can reinforce their arguments if necessary.

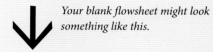

Your blank flowsheet might look something like this.

1st Proposition Constructive	1st Opposition Constructive	2nd Proposition Constructive	2nd Opp. Const./Opp. Rebuttal	Proposition Rebuttal
1st point A: R: E:	Refute	1st point A: R: E:		
2nd point A: R: E:	Refute	2nd point A: R: E:		

Understanding your flowsheet

You can see in the sample flowsheet above that there are six speeches, but only five columns. This is because the last two opposition speeches (second opposition constructive and opposition rebuttal) are given one after the other. It is basically one long speech, but given by two people.

What to listen for

As you listen to speakers, you need to write down the way they define their topic and their points—try to list the ARE (assertion, reason, evidence) of their arguments. Make sure you are as neat as possible. You need to list all the important facts, and not run out of room. You might need to practice this ahead of time.

How to fill out your flowsheet

As you take notes on multiple speakers, you will probably find that speakers do not give their speeches perfectly—they don't line up their arguments point for point with previous speakers. Rather, you will need to force your notes to do this for you.

Your notes on each speech should line up with the notes on the other speakers. You will also need to list any new points that the sides bring up as the debate progresses.

As the debate goes on and you fill more space on your flowsheet, you might find it helpful to connect some ideas across the paper. Arrows are a helpful way to do this.

For example, perhaps several of your opponents' ideas can be refuted as a group. If you connect these together with arrows on your flowsheet, this will help you remember to make these connections when it is your team's turn to speak, rather than taking the time to refute them individually.

1st Prop Cons	1st Opp Cons	2nd Prop Cons	2nd Opp Cons/ Opp Reb	Prop Reb
Dogs better than cats	Cats better than dogs			
1. More responsive to humans than cats, so make better pets.	Cats affectionate but less demanding. Easier pets than dogs for elderly and working people.	Dogs loyal to owners. Cats show little loyalty.		
2. Dogs more obedient and controllable.	Cats don't need obedience training. Don't need to be walked on leashes.	Walking dogs encourages physical exercise. Dog owners healthier. Statistics (quote) to prove.		
3. Can be trained to do work.	Cats safer family pets. Dogs can be aggressive. (Quote attack statistics.)	Dogs can do useful work (guide dogs, police dogs, etc.).		

Using your flowsheet

When it comes time for the representatives from each side to make final speeches, they need to know what has been said before. These are the speeches that will summarize the previous speeches and point out why either side should win. This is where note taking is critical: good notes can equal a won debate.

When you can properly listen and take notes during a debate, you can capture your opponents' arguments (or lack of arguments) and use them for your side. Let's say you notice that the opposition side forgets to refute your second argument. You can now tell the judge that is because they have no refutation on this very important point. Your rebuttal speaker could use this to help win the debate.

There are other times when a speaker will forget to complete a thought or use the wrong word to describe something. With good listening and proper flowing, you can easily take advantage of this error and ask questions that show your opponents' lack of preparation.

Try to avoid taking too many notes! This can lead to confusion and muddled thinking.

Practice your technique

Practice is the only way to improve your note-taking skills. One of the best practices for flowing is to take notes on the evening news or political debates on the TV.

Have a friend read out a list of names, numbers or ingredients. Tell them to read the lists quite slowly at first, then increase the speed. Practice making notes of all the items on the list, then read the list back to see how many you have managed to note down clearly.

You could also get a friend to read out lists of assertions, such as "Watching TV makes us stupid." "Zoos are prisons for animals." or "Teachers give us too much homework." Practice making short notes of each assertion, then check if you can read them back.

Getting it Wrong

Some people say that they prefer to take their own style of notes and that flowing is unnecessary. This is not true. Flowing is an excellent way to keep the debate organized. The method has been perfected over many years to enable you to be a better debater.

Team effort

Don't get disheartened if flowing feels more difficult than you think it should be. Making really effective notes takes practice. The first several times you flow debates you will probably find that you've missed points, written down too much or too little, or just got lost.

This is why everyone on your team needs to take notes. When you all compare notes, the combination of your efforts will probably cover pretty much all the important points that have been made. And remember, the better your notes are, the more likely you are to win.

Getting it Right

To keep your notes as short as possible, focus on keeping track of the main ideas and arguments. Don't try to write down everything. If you miss something, don't worry, focus on getting the next argument.

Remember these hints for neat note taking:

TIP

- Use black ink and make sure you have a spare pen or two.

- Take a large notepad to use for your notes.

- Use short forms of words to keep your notes clear and brief, such as opp. for opposition or 1st for first.

- Practice using symbols and use lines and arrows to make links between arguments clear.

QUIZ

DEBATING SKILLS

1) **Listening is an important skill for debating because:**
   a) you can overhear your opponents whispering.
   b) it gives you something to do during the debate.
   c) it allows you to better counter your opponent and build better arguments for your side.

2) **Flowing is:**
   a) only important for experienced debaters.
   b) a form of torture.
   c) a skill that can help you win a debate.

3) **Knowing logical fallacies can be helpful because:**
   a) it will give you ideas on how to sculpt your speech.
   b) teachers like to see you have memorized information.
   c) it will let you know what to avoid.

4) **A good debate speech is:**
   a) a single disconnected event.
   b) a pre-written speech.
   c) one part of a continuous 6-speech performance with clear arguments and counter-arguments.

To Sum Up

Debating is not just an interesting and "fun" activity. Regular debating will help you to improve your communication skills and increase your self confidence. It will also teach you to research a topic thoroughly, to pay close attention to detail, to express yourself clearly, and to listen carefully to the views of others.

TEAMWORK

Remember that you are working as a team. Be sure to share your ideas and knowledge with other team members, and encourage them to do the same. Listen to what they have to say. You are all out to win the debate, so plan your debate strategies together—making best use of each team member's strengths and ideas.

Research and ARE

The foundation of becoming a successful debater is doing your research. Ask yourself questions about your topic, and then hit the books and Internet. As you become more familiar with your topic, define and narrow its words and possible meanings. The more you have thought about all of this ahead of time, the more prepared you will be during a debate.

Once you know your topic, think about all the possible arguments either side of the debate could make. Remember that you won't know which side of the debate you are on

until shortly before the debate starts. Strengthen these arguments by thinking in terms of ARE (assertion, reason, and evidence).

Remember that a good speech begins with an attention-grabbing introduction and ends with a strong conclusion. Also think in terms of how you can refute these arguments. The strongest refutations use the four-step method of refutation—forming a refutation by using "They say," "But," "Because," and "Therefore."

Practice makes perfect!

Preparing on paper is not enough— you also have to think in terms of your performance. Practice, practice, practice to get over any nervousness about public speaking. Cure those nervous habits and learn to speak and present yourself in the most self-confident way possible.

Once it is time to debate, you can put all of your preparation to the test. Good research and sample arguments, rebuttals, and outlines will make you feel more at ease because you are so well prepared. Make strong, well-organized speeches. Use your knowledge of the topic to ask tough questions and offer POIs that show how you and your team are better informed and prepared than your opponents.

Keep listening

Make sure to use your listening skills during the debate. By keeping an accurate flowsheet of the debate, you will know exactly what arguments and refutations have been made. This will help you make your own arguments

and refutations better, while also helping you find flaws such as fallacies in your opponents' speeches.

Hopefully you will use the ideas in this book to become a poised, confident, and able speaker. It will take practice to master all of these skills and techniques, but doesn't everything take practice? Remember that debate should be fun. You might win and you might lose, but you should always have fun!

Debating is a team effort. Sharing research and ideas, practicing arguments and making constructive criticisms will make you stronger as a team.

QUIZ

SO YOU WANT TO DEBATE?

For page 19

- If you answered mostly a's:
  Your understanding of even the most simple terms is incomplete and sometimes downright wrong! You need to understand the concepts and principles more thoroughly if you are going to be a good debater.

- If you answered mostly b's:
  You have taken the time to understand the basic concepts thoroughly. You're ready to move on and learn more. Well done!

- If you answered mostly c's:
  You're a little overconfident in your approach. You feel your way is best and you haven't taken the time to understand key concepts and tried and tested methods.

QUIZ

DEBATING SKILLS

For page 47

- If you answered mostly a's:
  You're still a little overconfident. You think you know all the answers but you have misunderstood some important concepts.

- If you answered mostly b's:
  It's tricky to know if you have misunderstood or you are just not taking things seriously! If you want to be a good debater, you'll need to try harder.

- If you answered mostly c's:
  You understand how to construct a debate, the skills you need, and the pitfalls to avoid. You also have a clear understanding of all the principles. You're going to be a debating star!

20 THINGS TO REMEMBER

1. Be well informed. Read the newspaper or listen to the news so you know what's going on in the world. It could come up in a debate later.

2. Define and narrow your topic. Try to make sure you have thought of every way to approach it.

3. Remember that you won't know until the last minute which side of the debate you will be arguing. Prepare both sides of the topic backward and forward.

4. Do your research. Knowing your topic will make for a better debate, calm your nerves, and make you look really smart, too!

5. As you do your research, take good notes. Prepare your notes with your teammates so that everyone is thinking along similar lines.

6. When planning arguments, remember to use "ARE" (assertion, reason, evidence). Make sure that all of the points you make use this format.

7. While thinking of refutations, remember to use the four-step method of refutation ("They say," "But," "Because," and "Therefore").

8. Practice, practice, practice. You can never get too much practice.

9. Act confident. Even if you're not, it is essential that you pretend to be. With time and practice, you really will feel confident.

10. Remember to slow down and breathe when you are speaking. Pronunciation, speed, volume, word choice, and eye contact all help you to be more poised.

11. Leave "Amandas" at the practices. These filler words, such as "um" and "ah," get in the way of a quality speech.

12. Become aware of your nervous habits and avoid them during a speech. Develop helpful nonverbal skills such as strong gestures for emphasis.

13. Nothing starts off a good speech like a good opening line. A closing line is also important, as it will be the last thought you can leave with the judge.

14. A well-structured speech can help you with your speaking. Even better, the judge can follow what you are saying.

15. Think in terms of quality, not quantity. It is better to have three or four quality assertions than ten or twelve weak or unconvincing points.

16. Develop your ability to offer good Points of Information (POIs). Also be prepared to answer a few yourself.

17. Listen carefully to everything that is said in the debate.

18. Taking good notes by flowing a debate is critical to your success. It is hard to refute your opponents if you cannot remember what they said.

19. Be a competitor, but also be a good sport.

20. Have fun!

Further Information

You can find out more about debating through books, websites, and other resources. Here are some helpful places to start.

WEBSITES

This website lists a variety of common fallacies.
http://onegoodmove.org/fallacy/toc.htm

Learn more about phonetics (how different words sound) at this website.
www.fonetiks.org

This website offers a database of tongue twisters to practice.
www.geocities.com/Athens/8136/tonguetwisters.html

BOOKS

Davidson, Josephine. *The Middle School Debater*. Bellingham, Wash.: Right Book, 1997.

Kline, Jason. *Public Forum Debate*. New York: Rosen, 2007.

Meany, John, and Kate Shuster. *Speak Out! Debate and Public Speaking in the Middle Grades*. New York: International Debate Education Association, 2005.

Humes, James C.. *Speak Like Churchill, Stand Like Lincoln: 21 Powerful Secrets of History's Greatest Speakers*. New York: Three Rivers, 2002.

ORGANIZATIONS

The Middle School Public Debate Program
http://middleschooldebate.com/index.htm
Learn more about the MSPDP debate format at this site.

The International Debate Education Association
www.idebate.org
This website of the International Debate Education Association promotes debate and debate clubs throughout the world.

DEBATE FORMATS

The following is a list of common debate formats:

Australasia: Two teams of four speakers each debate a topic that is usually specific to the region.

extemporaneous: Two teams of two speakers debate. There is usually very little preparation time given.

European Youth Parliament: A large debate in which many speakers can speak on the topic (usually a government issue). It is similar to the Student Congress and Model United Nations in the United States.

Karl Popper: Two teams of three speakers debate. Topics are announced beforehand. This is popular in Eastern Europe and Central Asia.

Lincoln-Douglas: Two speakers compete against each other over a set resolution focused mainly on philosophical values.

mock trial and moot court: Debates that usually simulate real court trials.

Model United Nations (UN): Students simulate being members of the United Nations, the international organization of cooperative countries, and try to solve international problems through speeches and cooperation.

parliamentary: Teams of two or three speakers debate. The topic can be given weeks before the event or sometimes 20 minutes prior to the debate. The Middle School Public Debate Program (MSPDP) is an example of this format.

policy: Two teams of two speakers debate on a topic that is given once a year. The topic is usually a resolution that calls for a change in policy by a government.

public: Two teams of two speakers debate a topic that is given only 15 minutes prior to the debate.

Student Congress: Students simulate being members of the U.S. Congress and debate issues such as new bills and resolutions.

GLOSSARY

Amanda filler word used during speaking, such as "um" or "er"

argument point that supports your side or destroys the point of an opponent

assertion claim or positive statement or declaration

constructive speech speech that presents the points that build up your case

counter challenge or oppose an argument

counterclaim statement that says the opposite of something

credible reliable source for factual information

cross-examination interview with someone that challenges or questions what the speaker said previously

defendant person or organization accused of a crime in a court of law

dilemma argument that has two or more possible solutions

domain (on the Internet) section of website addresses that share the same suffix (ending). For instance, .com.

emphasis use of pitch or tone to stress a word or phrase

evidence statistic, quote, or piece of actual information that supports one or more of your points

fallacy faulty logic

flowsheet long, rectangular piece of paper separated into five columns. It is used specifically for taking notes for each speaker during a debate.

format set of guidelines, or way to give a speech or take notes

impromptu an activity done without preparation

inflection change in tone of voice

monotone using only one tone

nonverbal not related to speaking

opposition team arguing against the topic

Point of Information (POI) short question or statement that is asked or said during an opponent's speech. It is often used to clear a misunderstanding, to question the other team's logic, to ask about the team's reasoning, or to state information that proves the other team wrong.

poise dignified, self-confident manner

proposition team arguing for a topic

prosecution (in a law court) the side who is accusing a person or organization of committing crime

reasoning logical explanation of the presented points, or showing why a point is beneficial to your team's argument

rebuttal speech speech that rebuts, or tries to prove another speech false or incorrect

refutation presenting an argument, logic, or evidence that disproves or tears down an opponent's point

roadmap brief outline of the speech a speaker is about to give

specialized vocabulary special terms used in a particular subject area

valid worthwhile or meaningful

verbal related to speaking

Index